No Salami Fairy Bread

Also by Beatriz Copello
Women, Souls and Shadows, Bemac Publications, Sydney
Forbidden Steps Under the Wisteria, Abbott Bentley
A Call to the Stars (translated into the Chinese language),
Crown Publishing Company Ltd, Taiwan
Meditations at the Edge of a Dream, Glass House Books,
Interactive Publications
Under the Gums' Long Shade, Bemac Publications
Lo Irrevocable del Halcon, Bemac Publications
Witches, Women and Words, Ginninderra Press
Beyond the Moons of August, University of Wollongong,
Thesis Collections

Beatriz Copello

No Salami Fairy Bread

Author's note

I wrote this book not as the poet that I am today but as the poet I was in 1971. My knowledge of the language then was limited, so I wanted *No Salami Fairy Bread* to reflect that certain innocence of language and life.

This project has been assisted by the Commonwealth Government through the Australia Council, its arts funding and advisory body.

No Salami Fairy Bread
ISBN 978 1 76109 539 9
Copyright © text Beatriz Copello 2023
Cover image: Ally Designs

First published 2023 by
GINNINDERRA PRESS
PO Box 3461 Port Adelaide 5015
www.ginninderrapress.com.au

Contents

They Think They Are Right	7
I Told My Friends	8
I Am Too Old	9
Where Are We Going, Mum?	10
Dolls	11
Santiago	12
Talking to Myself	13
Migrants	14
'Let's Take a Photo!'	16
Landing	17
Breakfast	18
'Where Have You Brought Me?'	19
The Statue	21
What Have I Done?	22
A Rented House	23
A Painter's Palette	24
Out of My Body	25
A Suitable Job	27
Shopping Expedition	29
Night Shift	31
On the Way Home	32
An Old Spirit	34
I Now Have Two Friends	36
Why	38
A Weekend Free	39
Camp Cove	44
Morning Tea	46
I Want to be Rich	47
Defiance	49
Chapattis and Biryanis	50

An Accident	52
Another Night	53
A Lift Home	55
Sadness	56
Intonations From a Disgruntled Husband	57
Intonations From a Would-be Lover	58
Confession to the Man Who Wears Boots	59
An Affair	60
A New Job	62
Guilt	63
It is Love	65
It's Time	66
Morning Drama	68
A Visit to the Doctor	69
The Truth Was Under the Bed	70
Piss Off	73
An Apology	74
A Weekend Filled With Tears	75
Farewell My Love	76
Another Goodbye	77
Alberta Street	78
I Learnt	79
Looking Back	80
Acknowledgements	82

They Think They Are Right

They come in the night
their eyes shining
through their hoods.
They believe they are right
and blindly
follow orders.
They think they are just,
fair men of virtue,
they do it for their country
to weed out the bad
they write the rules
they distort ideas
their toys are guns and knives.
Their mission is sacred,
they say as they kill.
Subversives they call them.
Women are raped
abused and tortured
and all is done
in the name of their country.
Property destroyed, taken,
sold as war trophies,
the intellectuals, the artists
are maimed and burned
sometimes dumped in a river
their feet bound
with wire and stones.

Sometimes there are
mock executions,
systematic torture:
la picana, la banderita
well refined TORTURE methods
to destroy the ideals
of those who demand
justice and freedom.

I Told My Friends

I told my friends I was leaving,
I couldn't remain in a country
where my words were judged
by my beliefs and ideas.
I couldn't live in a place
where art was suffocated
gagged and controlled.
I told them, during a cold
and windy night,
in our secret meeting place,
while reading our poems
written with angry words
and dreams of freedom.
'I've heard of writers
who disappeared, were imprisoned,
questioned and judged,
their houses raided and robbed.
'I'm frightened,' I said.
Not a word was uttered,
and with their heads down
they left the writers' corner
behind the friendly pub.

I Am Too Old

'We are going to Australia.
Will you come with us?'
'I am too old to go!'
'Please come with us.
I'll miss you.'
'I am too old to go!'
'I'll be lonely without you.'
'I am too old to go!'
'My daughters will need
their old, old grandmother.'
'How far is that place…
Australia?

Where Are We Going, Mum?

'Where are we going, Mum?'
'We're going to a land where the people are free...
where no one cares if you are from the left or the right.
Mummy will be able to paint the *Che Guevara*
as she sings "The International", she will be able
to read Marx and Lenin and the life of Eva Peron.'
'What is the name of that country, Mum?'
'That country, my darling, is Australia!'

Dolls

'Mum, I want to take to Australia
my doll Pepita and the one that walks,
also, the one that wees and of course
my Batman and Robyn
'cause I'll marry them when I grow up
…and I want to take my Mickey Mouse
and my Donald Duck and you know
I cannot sleep without my teddy.'
'Only one doll you can take.
You must choose with great care.'
'I hate Australia. I don't want to go.
I want to keep all my dolls.
Why can't we stay here?'

Santiago

Santiago was a rabbit
a rabbit who behaved
and believed he was a cat.
On cold winter nights
he scratched at the door
to get into the warm
and welcoming kitchen.
Santiago jumped on beds,
slept on our laps
he liked to be tickled
be brushed and be loved.
I think I saw tears
in Santiago's eyes
when, with a sad and
trembling voice I told him,
'I am sorry, Santiago.
We cannot take you with us.
in Australia you are vermin.'

Talking to Myself

How many books can I fit into a suitcase?
How many farewell presents? Dresses? Photos?
Fold everything into small bundles,
squash the painting of the Spanish ancestor.
Throw away sheets, blankets and towels.
In this pocket I can fit a vase.
I wonder how much space
is left in my suitcase for all my dreams?

Migrants

I thought of the old couple
who from a sepia- coloured photo
presided over all my grandparents' parties.
I imagine them at the port
of Buenos Aires, so far from Genoa,
arriving in Argentina,
seven children in tow
…and a few liras!
Migrants from Italy
clutching a dream,
for a better life.
It was now my turn
to leave the Americas
dragging my family
into my own wild chimera,
escaping from an uncertain future,
escaping from real
and imagined dangers,
searching for adventure,
fortune, fame and freedom.
Wanting to dip myself
in the blue and calm sea
that I have seen in the newsreels.
I have heard so many things
about the wild Australia.
'Land free for those willing to work it,
seven men for every woman,
children needed to build
a strong country,
a lamb at the foot of a lion.

Kangaroos and koalas
roaming in the dusty streets,
and pubs where only tough
bearded men drank.'
So much to do
to build the land
of milk and honey!

'Let's Take a Photo!'

'Let's take a photo, for posterity,' said the husband.
Six people, different ages, heights and build
smiled at the camera which froze for ever
that moment in time, a few minutes before
boarding the plane that brought them
to the magical land of Oz!
The grandmother in one hand held
the rosary beads she prayed with
for sixteen hours to save the plane
from a certain crash. With the other hand
she embraced the smallest girl
whose charming dimples and smile
is admired by everyone. The young couple,
cheek to cheek and with defiance
posed for the photo. She wears a mini
and sandals with a big daisy. His long brown hair
contrasts with his bright green shirt.
Flared pants and a handbag complete his outfit.
Both their right hands are raised
flagging the peace sign.
The oldest daughter – only six
looks at Mummy to copy her pose and posture
…and with her cowboy hat, blue jeans,
checked shirt and thumbs firmly grabbing her belt
she looks beyond the camera, beyond the husband,
beyond the present to a time
when dreams become a reality.

Landing

Beyond South America and the USA
beyond Europe and Asia stands Australia
the country that is welcoming us.
Excitement is written all over our faces
and we crowd around a window of the landing plane.
The girls look forward to new toys, sweets and visits
to the famous Taronga Zoo. Grandma is thrilled
the plane didn't crash, the powerful beads
and her prayers has seen us safely to our destination.
The husband wants more photos and pushes everyone away.
The young seventies couple are planning a family.
I, the dreamer, the wife, the young mother, the poet
write in my mind a thousand poems
about the beauty of Sydney from above.
Soon I will live in a house with a red roof,
soon I will feel the salt from the sea,
soon I will step into a new life.

Breakfast

The brightness of the day woke me up.
Seven o'clock – Westbridge Hostel.
A warm, gum-perfumed breeze
followed me to the packed dining room.
There were no continental breakfasts,
no croissants, nor omelettes,
instead, crispy cereals
served with tinned fruit
which soon became a soggy mess.
Greasy sausages sizzled
on the hot plate, lamb cutlets
which made me dry retch,
but I was grateful, so grateful.
Fast hands dish out the unusual food.
I hear the loud voices of Babel
as I convince my daughters
that the food is delicious.
'They all speak funny!'
says the little one
pointing a greasy finger
at the neighbouring tables.

'Where Have You Brought Me?'

Westbridge Hostel

'Sister, where have you brought me?
I sleep in a tin shed, on a hard bed,
under starched sheets and grey thin blankets.
I hate the food, the crowded dining room,
and the loud parents with their screaming children.

'Sister, where have you brought me?
The employment officer sent me
to Smith's chips and Kelloggs,
but sorry, Sis, I'm no good
for factory work. "Overqualified.
Too well dressed," the manager said
as he shook his head with a look
that I thought it said, "She is mad."

'Sister, where have you brought me?
No one speaks Spanish
and I don't speak English!
I ask people to repeat
what they are saying
and what do they do?
They shout at me
thinking I'm deaf.
Someone nearly punched me
because I looked at him.

'Sister, where have you brought me?
The flies follow me everywhere
the heat is unbearable
no bidets in the toilet
no swimming pool or maids,
no one sells gelato and I cannot get
an espresso after dinner.

'I lost the heels of two pairs of shoes
and we have no car to go around in.
Sister, where have you brought me?'

The Statue

As I walk around the streets
of Villawood near the hostel
I remember a statue which
stands in Rosario, facing
the river that embraces the city.
A gesture of gratitude to the
thousands of migrants that came
to Argentina *to fare la America*
A young skinny man, moulded in bronze
gazes forever towards the sea,
towards where all his ancestors
have lived and died. Over one shoulder,
with a careless attitude, he carries
his coat. One hand in his pocket
and his back a bit arched.
A migrant, honoured and respected.
I cross a road without looking,
and a man who nearly ran me over
hangs out of his car window and shouts,
'You bloody wog, get off the road!'
There is a statue in Rosario…

What Have I Done?

When I can no longer hear
the kookaburras laughing,
when I no longer feel
the sea breezes
cooling the heat of my body,
when I no longer have sand
in my hair and salt on my skin
when the paper boy has put
his whistle to rest and
the milkman delivers his cargo,
replacing empty bottles
with ones wearing silver tops
tops which the magpies tear
to drink the precious milk
when everyone is asleep in the house,
I lie in bed, as if shrouded
by the clean new sheets.
I am dead to my past,
alive in the present
breathing in new sensations,
excitement, surprises
the joy of the new.
…and with fright I shiver
as I ponder, 'What have I done?'
I have dragged my whole family
into a world so foreign
so different, so unusual and
to appease myself
I number in my mind
the pluses of this country.

A Rented House

We have a new house by the sea, in Ray Avenue – Vaucluse
where the rich and powerful live I have been told.
We are so lucky I was able to convince the old lady
that we did not have money now but
we all were going to find work very soon.
'I'll give you cheap rent, you all look OK,
not like some migrants,' she said,
as she shook our hands and gave us the keys.
How lucky! How lucky! A house by the sea!
Shinny red roof, carpet throughout and very old furniture
in a grand and formal style. Rooms and more rooms,
and a kitchen to cook for an army. The old lady's sister
had lived there until death. I gently touch everything, and
my fingertips read a glorious past, of ladies in gloves
and men with top hats. 'I can feel the vibes of the past,'
I said to my sister closing my eyes and with sarcasm she answered,
'You know you are mad! Don't you? You live in a world of your own.'
I told the girls and they believed me. The night before
they have seen a ghost bathed by moonlight reading a paper.
We are not scared of spirits…and holding hands
the three of us ran into the garden and rolled
on the fresh lawn as the ants tickled our feet.

A Painter's Palette

Colours which appeared to be mixed at random
yet they portray a certain order,
in my new life I see an orderly chaos in which nature
has carefully sprinkled a beauty that matches
the one created by people. The Opera House, the Cathedral,
the Mint, Parliament House…and the ever-moving sea
blue, green, grey, Hyde Park and the Botanical Gardens.
Trees everywhere, red roofs, newness and cleanliness.
Open spaces that swallow me and reflect my insignificance.
I told the girls, 'Australia has a private sun, which paints in gold
the houses, the plants, the lawns, the boats, and the harbour.'
My new 'old' house is adorned with hydrangeas, masses of
purple and pink which I cut to put in my bedroom.
We walk down Pitt Street, turn into Market, follow George Street,
and we reach Circular Quay. 'Where are the people?'
we curiously wonder. Roast dinners and sport.
Only we walk in the city on a Sunday afternoon in 1971.

Out of My Body

…and I'm back in Rosario
I walk on the familiar streets.
There is a friend
she walks towards me
but she doesn't see me.
I'm but a ghost who in the night
returns to the towns
where her heart is buried.
…and I saunter in the park
where I gave my first kiss
I visit the school where I sat
on hard wooden benches
where my fingers froze
in winter mornings.
I am back in Rosario,
where my hands
wrote poems on walls
and my mind created
dreams and paper flowers.
The lonely road that leads
to my father's tomb I walk,
and count the stones
covered by moss.
My house, how empty it appears
now that strange voices
echo behind its walls.
How sad my garden looks
now that I no longer
tend to its flowers.

Bells ring, perhaps the church
where my parents married.
No! No! It's the alarm clock,
time to confront new challenges,
time to bury my face within the pages
of the *Sydney Morning Herald*
with English–Spanish dictionary at hand,
my search for a job commences.

A Suitable Job

Scarba House for Children

Lady luck was again on my side
at last, a suitable job.
No factory or plant,
no cleaning or cooking,
no job for the unqualified.
My teaching papers
like a flag I waved,
my English was not so bad,
my looks: acceptable
my presentation impeccable.
'Yes, indeed. Very suited,'
said the administrator
with a sideways smile.
Now, I care and love
a precious flock
like I once tended
my rose garden.
My new treasures
I bath and dress
play with them
and put to sleep.
Seven glorious flowers,
seven young children
abandoned by their mothers
ignored by their fathers.
I kiss and hug them
and teach them to use
their knives and forks
in a proper manner.

The other carers
laugh at me and call me mad
I heard them say,
'Who does this wog
think she is?'
The children in turn
teach me how to speak,
they ask me to bring them lollies
and beg me to take them out.
When I leave for home
they cry and they hang to my legs.
With my heart in pieces,
I drive home in my new car
a Morris on death bed
which I discovered
cost less when bought new.
At home I tell the girls,
'When you were just a sparkle,
just a soul without a body,
the gods and goddesses
gave you their blessings.
You have a family that loves you,
plenty of food on your plate,
warm clothes in winter
and a future in this marvellous
country – Australia!'

Shopping Expedition

With the trolley firmly gripped,
sauntering through the aisles
Mother anxiously shops.
This is not one of the friendly
neighbourhood shops where
she always recognises a bargain.
She is such a good shopper!
She knows when an apple is fresh
she knows how to chose bananas
cauliflowers, pumpkin or radishes.
She has always selected with care
the greenest and firmest vegies,
no tin foods with preservatives
no harming chemicals or colouring.
But this place is different
this is a SUPERMARKET,
where no one chats
about the weather or
the goods for sale.
There are no bakers
to tell you that the rolls
are at their best,
or greengrocers
to give you free
vegies for your soup.
…and all these tins
with cats on the front!

She chooses breadcrumbs
which turns out to be
chook food,
dry mustard which she mistook
for finely grated cheese.
I found her crying in the kitchen,
what she thought was
chocolate cream resulted in
something salty called Vegemite.

Night Shift

Two weeks of night shift:
I fold nappies, feed the babies
and wonder what my life
will be when I fully understand
what everyone is saying.
Nurses, sisters and carers
we have supper together.
They speak, they laugh,
now, they all look very serious.
Like the game 'Simon Says'
I do as they do, but sometimes
I laugh for too long, other times
I nod in agreement when the answer
should have been 'NO'.
I dream of the day I can
join in their jokes and tales.
Sister Applebe pats my back
and tells me I'm a good girl!
What have I done to deserve
such a comment?
They speak fast and
their lips never move
I say, 'Of course', 'Of course'
all the time, it seems to
go very well.
I dream of the day.

On the Way Home

The shift has ended at last
the children are all warm in bed
the cool air enters through
my thin, short uniform
'That uniform is too short!'
my husband had said
'That's how everyone
is wearing it,' I had replied.
Feeling good about myself
working and doing a good job
I fly home in my Morris
my chariot from hell.
A siren approaches me,
my god, the police!
I stop and shiver in fright
His presence brings bad memories
a young officer asks me,
'Is this a car or a war tank?'
Obviously, he didn't like the fact
that the Morris exhaust pipe
had a hole as big as the moon.
'This is a Morris car, officer.'
I reply in my best English.
He wants my licence now.
Still hands trembling
I pass to him my licence,
a plastic card which in Spanish
says that I can drive cars.

He did not like my card either,
he tells me he'll let me go,
but I need an Aussie licence
and the car fixed.
'If I see you again, and the car
is not repaired, and you don't
have a licence from here,
I'll give you a fine
you'll never forget.'
He hasn't jailed me,
thank god, and
he even smiled when
he sent me on my way.
The sun is rising
and the never tiring sea
waves and rests
on the cold sand.
On the last curve
of New South Head Road
I look again at the bay
I want to sleep with that image
colouring my dreams.

An Old Spirit

With a baby on my lap,
I doze and wake up several times,
tiredness overwhelms me,
the hours without sleep
leave a mark on my face
and my body wants to sleep.
Outside the wind raises
the dry leaves which career
towards the window
noisily hitting the glass.
A minuscule ray of light
has squeezed, through
the heavy velvet curtains,
a ray which lets me see
the room, the furniture
and the babies in their cots.
I saw her when I opened my eyes.
Was I dreaming of such beauty?
Metres and metres of blue organza
gathered around her waist,
tight to her breast
was the top of the dress.
Her blonde long hair
curled over her shoulders,
long silk gloves covered
her hands and half her arms,
a lonely black pearl drop
hung from a gold chain
around her slender neck.

There she stood
by the marble fireplace
an arm resting on the mantelpiece,
with a lace handkerchief
she dried her tears
which like stars shone
in the darkened nursery.
'Sister!' 'Sister!'
I scream with panic.
Sister Applebe enters the room,
firm steps on the polished
wooden floor. She has gone by now,
the spirit is not longer there.
'What's the problem?' Sister asks.
'I've seen a spirit'
I blurted, as my eyes
kept searching for the
woman by the fireplace.
Sister did not tell me
I must have been dreaming,
nor did she tell me I was crazy.
'She was the owner of
this house, her son was killed
in the war. She just
mourns forever. Don't tell
the others,' Sister explained,
and then she rested a finger
on her dry old lips.

I Now Have Two Friends

I now have two friends
they are young Sisters
from Scarba House.
They want to travel the world
they are keen to learn,
to argue, and to teach me
to speak as they do
when they are not at work.
'Strine' and 'ocker'
they called the way they converse.
Summer is at its peak.
A rostered day off, a day
away from the children:
Scarba's and my own.
No husband to watch
what I do or wear,
my eyes can wonder
all over the beach,
my top can be off,
and I can smoke
as much as I like.
'What is the name
of that *bird*?'
I ask my new friends.
'Which one, the blonde one,
or the one wearing
a one-piece?' asks
one of my friends.

I tell her I am not
referring to girls!
I am curious about
the grey and white birds
who move at ease
amongst all the bronzed
sun addicts. 'A seagull,'
explain Diedre and both
laughed for a while.
A handsome lifesaver
is now talking to them,
they all speak so fast.
Meantime I admire
his ample muscles,
his legs and arms, and
his face is not so bad.
But what a ridiculous hat!
Now, they all look at me,
they tell me he wants
to take me out for a drink.
I say, 'I'm sorry I am married.'
The sun is going down,
soon I will be home
to be with my family life.
'Why are you so quiet?'
they will all ask, and
I won't tell them why,
but I am sure I will be thinking
about the lifesaver
who wears the silly hat.

Why

Why do people marry?
Why do people become
prisoners of relationships,
children and family affairs?
Why do I have to tell
my husband where I go,
what I do and who have I seen?
Why do I have to consult him
if I want to study or change
my job which makes me sad?

A Weekend Free

Saturday Morning

We stroll through Double Bay
and admire the things
that one day we will buy.
My sister is worried
'I look too fat,' she says.
'You look pregnant,' I reply.
The coffee shop at the Roma Arcade
looks inviting and we enter
we order two cold beers.
'Ladies don't order beers
at this café,' whispers the waitress.
Sister and I look at each other
and insist that these two ladies
also would like peanuts with their beers.
Everything is too expensive
in Double Bay shops,
we want two hippie
dresses to wear tonight
so we head for Bondi Junction.
In a shop smelling of patchouli
we found the dresses
as well as head bands
with flowers and ribbons.

Saturday Night

Wearing our new dresses,
my sister's in orange tones
and mine in purple and gold,
we feel like two queens.
We buy two bottles of wine,
the friends who invited us
explained the meaning of BYO.
We arrive late to the party,
everyone jokes,
'There's no "Spanish" time
here in Australia!'
They say as they laugh.
They all are eating lasagne,
'A new dish from Italy
that everyone is cooking,'
said Diedre as she serves us.
After dinner, they all roll their own,
we take out our Dunhills out.
They pass their butts around
and I do the same.
They all laugh again,
and someone says,
'This is pot, man!'
I realise I had made a gaffe,
red to the root of my hair
I go to the toilet,
to check in my dictionary.

Pot? Pot? Pot?
The word is not there.
I look for Anne,
my other friend
and ask her to explain.
'Marijuana,' she says.
'You get high as a kite.
Come, I'll teach you how
to smoke it.'
I suck on the butt,
and send the smoke
deep into my lungs.
I pat my stomach,
three times with one hand,
and wait for the high.
The music I hear
is weird and loud,
each instrument
plays on its own,
the room spins around,
and the colours
my god! It is a rainbow.
Now, I feel I am afloat
and Cat Stevens sings
only for me. The dog on the couch
tells me tales and
I laugh and laugh until
my belly aches.

My husband does not approve,
from a corner he stares
at the faces I pull.
Sissy and her husband
have declined politely
to the offers of 'weed'
and stick to the wine.
Once at home, I am told
I am disgusting,
and what do I do?
I tell them the new sentence
that Diedre had taught me,
'All of you can get fucked!'

Sunday

I wake up to Tchaikovsky
playing too loud
on the second-hand record player.
With a thumping headache
I walk to the porch
where husband has been reading
since early this morning.
'Where are we going?'
I ask him, screwing
my face at the light
which is too bright.
'Nowhere,' he says
going back to his paper.
'In this country, everyone
goes out on a Sunday.
People go for drives, or picnics
or walks in the bush.'
'Today is Sunday,
we rest,' he states
with one finger waving.
'I'm going out with my daughters,'
I scream as we leave.

Camp Cove

Parking is a difficult task,
I search for a little space
to leave my Morris Minor,
the girls are excited
we all love the beach.
Finally, a spot.
Topless I sit on the sand
an eye on my book
the other on the girls.
They know how to swim
I taught them when they were
just out of their nappies
but I've been told
about the dangers of sharks.
'They have you for lunch,'
someone had cautioned me.
Baby oil on the skin,
the best for a suntan.
I wave my arms
they have gone too far out.
'Hello,' he says.
'Can I sit next to you?'
he asks. I look up
ready to answer
the handsome
blond Australian.

An answer was coming
when the girls appeared
as if from nowhere.
'Mummy! Mummy!
We're here,' they screamed
in unison and loud.
He picked up his towel,
which he had already
dropped on the sand
and with a sad smile said,
'Sorry, I thought
you were somebody else.'

Morning Tea

Tea and toast, cakes and biscuits,
a cigarette and a short rest.
In our 'Tarzan' English
us migrants from everywhere,
try to speak and answer the questions
from the Australian Sisters.
The young ones are patient
and repeat with care
their words and expressions,
the older Sisters ignore us
and natter to each other
laughing and giggling
perhaps at our accents.
I get upset at some
of the migrant women
everything in their country
is bigger and better.
'Why are you here?'
I recriminate with anger.
Australia is now my country
if they don't like it
they can all go back.
…and I get shitty when
they ask me if I miss 'HOME'.
'This is my home,'
I tell them with pride.

I Want to be Rich

Perhaps if I take
a job in the evenings
I soon will be rich,
then I'll be able
to study
to be a people's helper,
to be a psychologist.
'Look in the paper
under part-time jobs,'
Diedre advised me.
'Indian waitress needed.
East Indian Restaurant,
two evenings a week,
apply within.'
I believe that
with my black hair,
a red dot on my forehead
and a long hippie dress
I can pass for an Indian.
'You're not an Indian,'
the manager blurted.
'I don't think it matters,
I am South American.'
'What do you know
about curries and koftas?'
'Nothing so far,
but I'm such a quick learner.'
'But where is your sari?'
'I'll buy one tomorrow.'

'I'm John. You can start
next Monday,' he said
shaking firmly my hand.
'In my other job they call me
Nurse Copello, but you –
you can call me Miss Beatriz!'

Defiance

'Don't tell your in-laws
that you work as a waitress
dressed up as an Indian. They'll
think we have all gone mad.
…and your husband
he's so angry and annoyed.
Give up that silly job!'
Recriminated my mother.
'Mother, can't you understand
that I want to study
I want to help people
I need to earn money
to pay for university fees.'
'So then when you study
you'll never be home,
resentment and sorrow
will be the result.
Your husband will leave you,
your children will hate you.
You'll be left in your own.'
'I know what I want.
I know where I'm going,
don't worry about me.
Don't think I'm a child
Mum, I'm a grown-up now!'

Chapattis and Biryanis

I took the menu home
and studied the names
of the unusual food:
koftas and puris,
chapattis and biryanis,
curries hot or mild.
Wines red or white,
beer and whisky.
'Side dishes, madam?'
'Another bottle, monsieur?'
On Monday I will start,
I will wear a red sari
and a flower to match
in my long black hair.
On Monday
my feet can't be seen,
I fly from the kitchen
to the packed dining room
and back to the kitchen.
'I want more chapattis!'
'My curry is too hot!'
'Where's my water?'
'I asked for my bill
a long time ago.'
When I finish work
at two in the morning
my body aches from
the top of my head
to my little toe.

I count my tips and my pay,
if I continue to work
at least three nights a week
I will have soon
enough money
to pay for my fees.

An Accident

Two weeks of night shift,
six nights at the restaurant,
made me tired and moody
and I need to drive
my girls to school.
It is late and it is raining
I turn a curve at full speed.
Stupid and careless…
I did not see a young man
on his bike and hit him.
He rolls to the ground,
his bike next to him.
It's a Honda I notice
when I look at the mangled
mess I had made.
The girls scream and cry
I don't know what to do.
He is moving,
he raises his arms,
he is looks at me.
Thank god! He is alive!
'You failed to give way to the right!'
said the policeman who charged me.
It takes all my savings
to pay for his bike and the fine.
University starts shortly,
no money, no fees!
Another year it will take me
to save that much again.

Another Night

The first thing I noticed
were his boots and his scarf,
he works behind the bar
on Tuesdays and Thursdays.
On the first few encounters
we ignored each other,
we were too busy
to exchange pleasantries.
Today a rainy Monday night,
while I fold serviettes
he walks in as a client
and orders a curry.
I watched him as he
sprinkles his meal
with pure white coconut.
He is blond and his eyes
are blue as the sea in Bondi.
He is handsome and gentle,
and he smiles when he orders
another small bottle of beer.
'You're Miss Beatriz?'
he asks me and requests
more poppadums and bananas.
I stand next to him
while he finishes his meal.
We talk about him
we talk about me.
He says he was a lawyer,
who needs extra money.

'A lawyer!'
I exclaimed with surprised.
'No! Not a lawyer,
I am a bricklayer!'
he shouts. (A lot of people shouted at me when I did not
understand their English.)
'We'll talk more
one of these nights,
when we're not so busy,'
he said as he pays me.
As soon as he goes, I realise
I don't know his name.
For the next few days,
my mind is flooded
with the image
of the lanky barman
who wears black boots
and a flowery silk scarf.

A Lift Home

My Morris is dead,
I need a lift home.
I ask everyone
if they go near Vaucluse.
They all raise
their eyebrows
when they hear
I live in Vaucluse.
'No wonder the lady
wants us to call her
Miss Beatriz,' said
the wife of the cook.
They all laughed at the joke
which I did not understand.
The barman said he was pleased
to drive me home any time.
It was very difficult
to get into his truck
wearing a sari
and shoes with a platform.
He moved a big shovel,
other tools and some rugs
for me to sit next to him.
'Miss Beatriz, would you care
to go for a drive by the beach
before you go home?'
the tall sexy barman whispered
while revving his old battered truck.
Of course, I wanted to go for a drive
with the barman with the black boots!

Sadness

Sadness overwhelms me
I can no longer work at Scarba.
Every child's tear
every child's scream
every tantrum
hurts me like if a knife
has entered my heart.
I cried when they brought in
the battered twins,
I cried when Darren
left for a new home.
I cried when
they begged me
to take them with me.
I can't stand the children
being force-fed.
Next Saturday I will search
for a new job in the city.

Intonations From a Disgruntled Husband

'Keep a secure job,
jobs are hard to find.'
'That job at East India
it takes you away from home.'
'You must be crazy
to want to go back
to study and be
a university student again.'
'That money you're saving
should go to buy things
that we need in the house.'
'That dress that you are wearing
it's too short and too tight.'

Intonations From a Would-be Lover

'You're so beautiful, Miss Beatriz,'
he said and then asked my permission
to hold my cold hands.
'You're so clever, Miss Beatriz,
you're already a teacher and
you're saving to pay for your fees.'
'Miss Beatriz, you're so fast
with that tray full of dishes,
and I love the way you serve wine.'
'Miss Beatriz, your hair and eyes
are black as the night.'
'Miss Beatriz, would you mind
if I give you a kiss on the lips?'

Confession to the Man Who Wears Boots

My father died and
left us with nothing.
I married to solve
a financial situation.
It wasn't a marriage of love.
I married the man
who is now my husband
for money and protection.
He is eighteen years older than me
often people ask me
if he is my father.
I am embarrassed to tell you
but we never have sex,
he is always reading the paper,
he is either tired or sick.
He orders me around
and treats me as a child.
That is why I want to be free
That is why I want to divorce.

An Affair

He took a day off,
from his mortar and bricks.
He wanted to enjoy
a day at the beach.
Tamarama was crowded
for a Monday morning.
'I don't care for money,
but do you know how much
it costs me to have
this day next to you?'
he said as he rubbed
baby oil on my back.
I sighed and smiled.
We swam and we had
two pies and two beers
and then we drove
to his place in Bondi.
It was dark and dingy,
humid and cold,
the bed was unmade,
and there was
dog shit everywhere.
As soon as with passion
he took me into his arms
I forgot the mess and the stench
the dirty sheets and
the black smelly towels.
He kissed me with such ardour
that I believed I was floating.

We made love many times,
and after that afternoon
I believed that he was
the man of my life.

A New Job

'I have never seen
anyone so fast
with their maths.
I'll give you the job!'
Mr Frost said, as
soon as he finished
correcting the test.
'Your English doesn't matter,
you're the person we want.
Someone who can add and divide,
write our invoices and
charge or settle accounts
as fast as you can.
You can start as soon
as you want. Gilbeys will be
most happy to have you.'

Guilt

I am walking home from Rose Bay
I want to ponder
what happened today
at Bondi in his flat,
in his arms…on his bed…
Two emotions compete
in my mind. The pleasure I had
and the pleasures to come,
against the guilt
of having done
what I shouldn't:
I cheated on my husband.
I say to myself,
it is his fault,
he doesn't deserve me,
he is too bossy and
never makes love.
I am young and
need a young man.
The nuns teachings
begin to resurface:
I am…oh my god!
an adulterous woman!
What would my mother say
if she knew about the man
who wears boots and a scarf?

What would she say
about her lascivious daughter
who has not respected tradition,
religion and all the rest?
Would my children forgive me?
What would my husband do
if he knew about my deception?
Would I then be free
to do everything as I please?

It is Love

As my love increases
my guilt reduces.
We have been out for dinner,
to the movies and the zoo.
He gave me a hat
I gave him a scarf.
His place is now clean
his bed has new sheets,
the dog is being trained.
At home I tell them
'Well, the restaurant needs me.
It is called overtime.'
I'm hardly ever home
and I wonder when
will he ask me,
'Leave your husband,
bring the girls,
and move in with me.'
He says he loves me,
he says I am his life,
he adores me, he dreams of me.
'Each other we made for,'
I say as I breathe on his ear.
'We are made for each other,'
he corrects as he nibbles my neck.

It's Time

The Tea Lady is wearing
a big badge on her coat.
it says, 'IT'S TIME'.
I ask my workmates,
'What does it mean?'
'She's mad,'
one of them grunts,
and another retorts,
'She will vote Labor.
We Liberals don't like
Whitlam's talk or his promises.'
Next day, I anxiously wait
for the Tea Lady to come.
At ten we arrange
to meet at lunchtime.
We sit on the patio
of the pub next door
we drink beer and smoke.
She tells me about Whitlam,
his vision and dreams.
She also tells me
about Medibank,
the free health insurance,
about pensions and benefits,
and the most important of all
she tells me about no – university fees.
'You should know about Al Grassby
he is all for the "wogs".' I sigh
and explain, 'It's so difficult
to read the newspaper.

I can read books but the papers…'
She says she will teach me
about the Labor Party and its men.
She even promises to take me
to some of their meetings.
'They'll be happy,
they want people like you.'
I raise my eyebrows and ask
'People like me?'
'Yes, new Australian,' she says.

Morning Drama

Mother angry shouts at me
to come and get the girls
dressed for school or else.
The girls refuse to go to school.
'What's the problem?' I ask her.
They don't want to wear shoes.
They want to wear their hippie sandals
'…and the sandwiches we take to school,
are silly and stale. We want fairy bread,
or bread with Vegemite or peanut butter, and, and
and cookies made of cornflakes.'
I let them wear the sandals
to my mother's horror, who believes the teachers
will think we are peasants if the girls don't wear
their black leather shoes. I beg mother not to worry
and to the girls I promise that they will shortly have
all the fancy food they want for lunch.
I'd heard of Vegemite and peanut butter,
but not about 'fairy bread' and cornflake cookies?
The morning drama was temporarily solved.
As I shower I ponder, who will teach me
about this 'fancy food'.

A Visit to the Doctor

'Sister, I can't drive any longer,
my belly is too big, and besides
your English is a lot better than mine.
I have this itch between my legs
up there, you know?'
'You may have fungus there, and
of course, I will take you.
Let's check the Spanish dictionary.
We need to find out the
name for the place
where you are itching,
and the name for the itch.'
The doctor was helpful,
he spoke very slowly
when I did the translations,
and then we turned red,
we were very embarrassed,
the doctor was laughing
and he wouldn't stop.
I was so disappointed,
I thought I had the right words
when I said to the doctor,
'I believe my sister
has mushrooms in her crotch.'

The Truth Was Under the Bed

After we made love,
he rushed out,
to see a builder,
who promised him
work at a new site.
I had to be at the East India
by six sharp.
The owner had warned me,
'Not Spanish time.'
I dress in a hurry,
but where are my shoes?
I look to the right
of the big double bed.
I look to the left,
I look under the bed.
No! Those are not my shoes!
They are not suede,
they are not sandals,
they have no platform,
those are not my shoes!
I pick them up with disgust.
I soon recognise them
I know who owns these shoes,
they belong to the new
topless barmaid,
the one that works
when my lover
is not there.

I finally found
my own dammed shoes,
and I run next door
to the East India Bar.
'Have you slept next door?'
I asked her, as I noticed
her erect nipples.
'Oh, a few times,' she moaned
'Did you sleep with the barman?'
I clarified, my legs trembling
my mouth dry and
my heart dying.
'Well, yes of course.
Why? Are you having
an affair with him?'
She answers and asks
in one fast mouthful.
Now, I am angry,
it shows in my eyes,
I am spitting fire
as I state, 'Yes!
We are formally lovers!'

She looks at me with pity,
and rests her cold hands
on my naked shoulders
and coyly utters,
'You poor thing,
you took the affair
as a blessed wedding.
But you shouldn't have,
this is the seventies,
don't you know?'

Piss Off

A song from Cat Stevens
was playing in the restaurant
when he walked into the kitchen,
'Good evening, Miss Beatriz,'
he said as he pinched
my red cheeks.
'Don't touch me!'
I screamed as I pushed him away,
and then remembered what Diedre
had taught me to say
to reject unwanted advances:
'Piss off, you bastard!'
The kitchen went dead
all we could hear
was the oil frying away.
'Yes, piss off and leave me alone.
Go next door and warm the tits
of that topless barmaid.'
I exited slamming the door.

An Apology

'Miss Beatriz, it was true
when I said that I loved you,
but I never said I was going
to be faithful to you.
I'm single and free and
I enjoy the company of women.
What do you expect me to do
while you are at home
with your husband and children?
I'm sorry you're hurt,
it was not my intention
to be cruel or mean.
The barmaid means nothing,
it was just a quick fling.
I love you, Miss Beatriz
but you have a husband
and two children as well.
I couldn't forgive myself
if I deprived your girls
of their true father.
I grew up without mine
and I know what it means.
It is up to you to accept me
just as a lover,
without demands or
expecting to get married.
Miss Beatriz, I love you.'

A Weekend Filled With Tears

I cry as I clean on top of the fridge.
I cry as I bake cookies made with cornflakes.
I cry as I sprinkle bread with hundreds and thousands.
I cry as I drive
I cry as I breathe.
I cry as much as I can today is Sunday
I won't be able to cry any more the day after today.

Farewell My Love

In a way I am an old-fashioned girl,
respect and trust I expect from
the man I love. I cannot forgive him,
even if he says he loves me.
What he has to offer has no value.
How childish, how stupid I have been.
guilt has left me because I have not hurt anyone.
Farewell my barman! Farewell my love!

Another Goodbye

At the East India everyone has found out
that I had a lover. They laugh behind my back,
and joke about lovers that cheat.
I ignore them and I work as hard as I can,
cutting side dishes in the dark workroom
between the kitchen and the big restaurant.
I am trying so hard to ignore everyone
that I do not hear when someone walks in.
Suddenly I feel something hard
and hot against me. The man in charge
is pressing his 'thing' against my buttocks.
I scream and slap him, I throw at his face
coconut and bananas, a handful of chilli,
the pickled mango and a tub of yoghurt.
He is paralysed by my actions.
Before he reacts, I grab my big tray
and thump him with all my might.
I go to the kitchen and I shout to all,
my friend's famous words,
'Piss off, all of you bastards.'
Still holding the tray
in my trembling hands
I walk out of the East India
to never return.

Alberta Street

I go to Macquarie, the newest university,
to find out about enrolling in a course to study
to be a great shrink. (Diedre also taught me this word)
I now have all the papers. No fees! Free education!
Thanks to Whitlam and the Labor Party.
I walk around the campus, I admire the growing trees,
the buildings, and the modern paintings
at the grand library. Excited
I look forward to an intellectual future,
I go to the crowded canteen
to have a coffee and relax.
As I leave the amenities room
I notice a mauve-coloured sign:
WOMAN DO YOU WANT TO BE FREE?
I continue reading with interest:
COME TO A CONSCIOUSNESS
RAISING SESSION TONIGHT.
WE ARE HERE TO HELP YOU
UNDERSTAND LIBERATION.
SISTER COME TO OUR HOUSE
IN ALBERTA STREET.

I Learnt

… And I went to that session
and more, many more.
I learnt about exploitation,
about men's intentions,
their power, their control
and the way in which
women were oppressed.
I marched in the streets
carrying banners that said,
'NOT THE CHURCH,
NOT THE STATE,
LET WOMEN
CHOOSE THEIR FATE.'
The girls enjoyed the chanting
when I took them on our marches.
I shocked my husband,
my mother, my family
with all my new beliefs.
As time passed, I realised
that my life was only mine.
I packed a case for the girls and I,
and we left for a new life,
somewhere in Ryde,
near Macquarie: my uni
where I had been accepted
to study for a BA
majoring in Psychology.

Looking Back

Now that the papers that
say that I have
degrees, diplomas and masters
are somewhere forgotten
at the bottom of a drawer,
now that I believe I am free
and can do what I want
whenever I want,
now that the girls have grown up,
now that I have mastered the language
that gave me so many headaches,
now when my sister and her husband
are soon to be grandparents,
now that my ex-husband is married
to wife number four,
now that my mother is no longer with us,
now that I can call Australia my country,
now, today, I feel nostalgia
not for the past, but for the enthusiasm,
the motivation, the drive of that naive
young woman who opened her heart
to a new world and its people.

Acknowledgements

Some of these poems have been published previously:

Southerly: 'They Think They Are Right', 'I Told My Friends', 'I Am Too Old', 'Where Are We Going, Mum?', 'Dolls' and 'Santiago'

The Swallows, Australian-Hispanic Women Business Network, 2012: 'Talking to Myself'

The Muse Apprentice Guild: 'A Rented House'

www.ingramcontent.com/pod-product-compliance
Lightning Source LLC
Chambersburg PA
CBHW071027080526
44587CB00015B/2531